Fossils

Jill McDougall

D1635342

Contents

The Fossil Discovery Tour

Hello there! I'm Dr Dig, and I know lots of interesting things about fossils. Let's go on a fossil discovery tour!

a Tyrannosaurus rex skull fossil in rock

a Poplar leaf fossil

3

What Are Fossils?

Fossils are the **remains** of plants and animals that lived long ago. Fossils have lasted for thousands of years.

a fossilised fish skeleton

a fossilised tree stump

4

a fossilised
Triceratops skull

I just
love fossils.

5

Tough Stuff

Fossils are very old. Some are at least 10 000 years old. Some are millions of years old! Some fossils are parts of animals. The hard parts of animals' bodies make the best fossils.

You won't find fossil eyeballs or fossil ears. Eyeballs and ears **rot** in the ground or get eaten before they can become fossils.

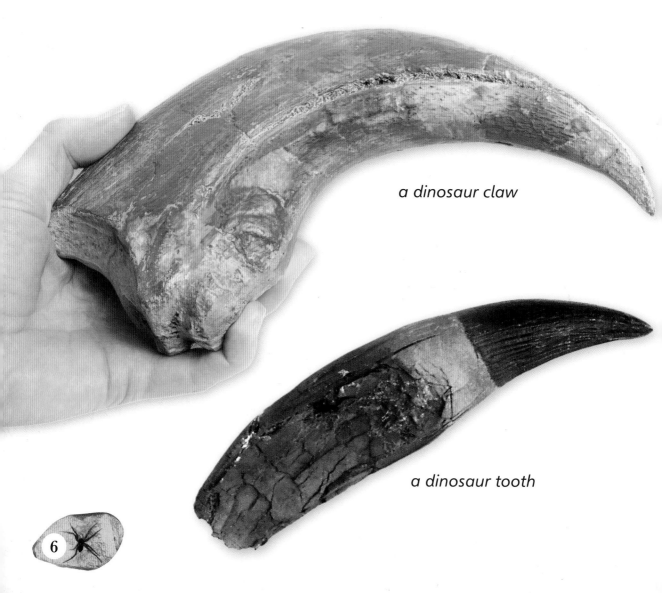

a dinosaur claw

a dinosaur tooth

Tough Stuff
(Great for making fossils)

shells
feathers
claws
bones
teeth

Soft Stuff
(Not good for making fossils)

skin
eyeballs
ears
noses
flesh

an Allosaurus skull

7

Trace Fossils

Not all animal fossils are body parts. Some fossils are marks that the animal left behind, like footprints or bite marks – or even poo! These kinds of fossils are called **trace fossils**.

These are fossilised tracks (traces) of an ancient worm, preserved in rock.

This fossil is dinosaur poo. Don't worry, it's not smelly any more!

This is a fossilised footprint
of a Tyrannosaurus rex.

How Fossils Are Made

From Fish to Fossil

Fossils can be made in different ways. Here's how a fish might become a fossil:

1. A fish dies in a lake. The soft parts of the fish rot.

2. Mud builds up over the bones.

3. The bones turn into rock.

4. The fish has become a fish fossil!

Stuck Forever

Some fossils look just the same as when the animal died.
This spider is a fossil.

*a fossilised
spider in amber*

gum seeping out of wood

Here's how it became a fossil:

1. The spider got stuck in tree gum.
It died.

2. Millions of years passed ...
The gum became hard.

3. It's a spider fossil!

Frozen Fossils

In cold parts of the world, some animals became **frozen fossils**. Here's how:

1. A **woolly mammoth** is walking on an icy lake.

2. Suddenly, the ice starts to crack.

3. The mammoth falls into the icy water.

4. The mammoth dies.

5. The mammoth freezes.

6. Thousands of years later, the ice melts.

skin

fur

7. The fossil lies on the ground. It still has fur and flesh, like eyeballs, because it was buried in ice.

Stone Trees

Did you know that trees can turn to stone?
Here's how:

1. The tree is buried in mud.

2. Millions of years pass …

3. The tree has turned to stone!

tree bark

tree rings

a cross-section of a fossilised tree

14

Leaf Fossils

Leaves can be fossils, too. Here's how:

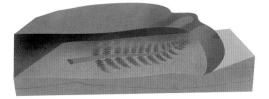

1. The leaf is squashed under mud.

2. The mud goes hard around the leaf. Millions of years pass …

leaf veins

a fossilised leaf imprint

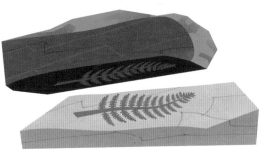

3. The leaf rots away. We see its **imprint** in the stone.

Big and Small

Some fossils are small enough to fit inside this 'o'.

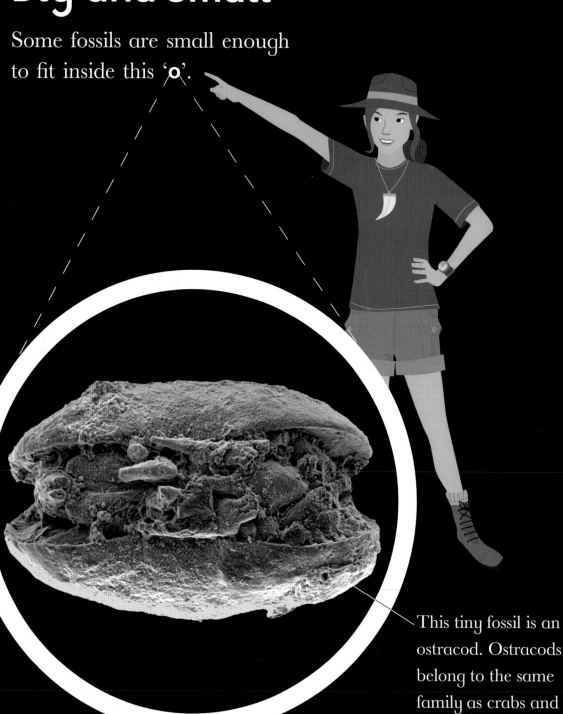

This tiny fossil is an ostracod. Ostracods belong to the same family as crabs and lobsters.

Some fossils are very big! This huge sea creature lived in the time of the dinosaurs. But it is not a dinosaur. It is a sea reptile.

June 18 2008

Published in Association with the National Fossil Museum

FOSSIL NEWS

Fossil Sea Monster Found!

June 2008: The fossil of a sea monster was found today in Norway. It lived 150 million years ago!

The huge creature was 15 metres long – that's about the same as five elephants standing end-to-end. Scientists have named the creature "Predator X". They believe that its mouth was so big, it could eat a small car.

Finding Fossils

Fossils can be found in all sorts of places:

- on a beach
- in a desert
- on a mountain
- in a cave.

Fossil hunters have to take care as they dig. They don't want to break the fossil. They might use a brush or a toothbrush to clean earth around a fossil.

the fossil

This is the fossilised imprint of an ammonite shell.

The Fossil Cave

Caves are exciting places to explore, especially if you find lots and lots of fossils.

In 1969, fossil hunters found a very special cave in Australia. The cave has a hole in the roof. Long ago, animals fell into the hole and died. Over thousands of years, more and more animals fell in, until their bones reached the cave roof!

The fossil hunters were amazed at all the different types of fossils they found in the cave.

Victoria Fossil Cave, Australia

20

original entrance

a cross-section of the fossil cave

21

Fossil Secrets

Fossils tell us secrets about life on Earth, millions of years ago. They can tell us how animals have changed. The elephant used to look more like a pig. How do we know? From fossils, of course!

Moeritherium
50 million years ago

Phiomia
35 million years ago

Gomphotherium
20 million years ago

Deinotherium
2 million years ago

Asian Elephant
Today

Dinosaur Fossils

No one has ever seen a dinosaur but we know a lot about them from their fossils. Let's take a look. This fossil is a Tyrannosaurus rex.

This fossil shows us just how big T. rex was! T. rex was 12.8 m long and 4 m tall at the hips.

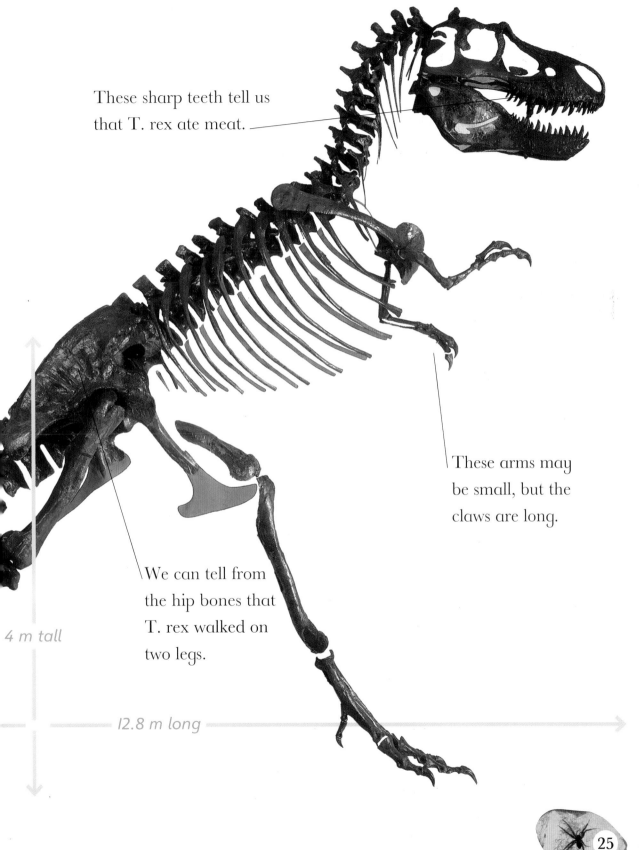

These sharp teeth tell us that T. rex ate meat.

These arms may be small, but the claws are long.

We can tell from the hip bones that T. rex walked on two legs.

4 m tall

12.8 m long

Make a Fake Fossil

Trick your friends with your very own fossil!

Here's what you need:

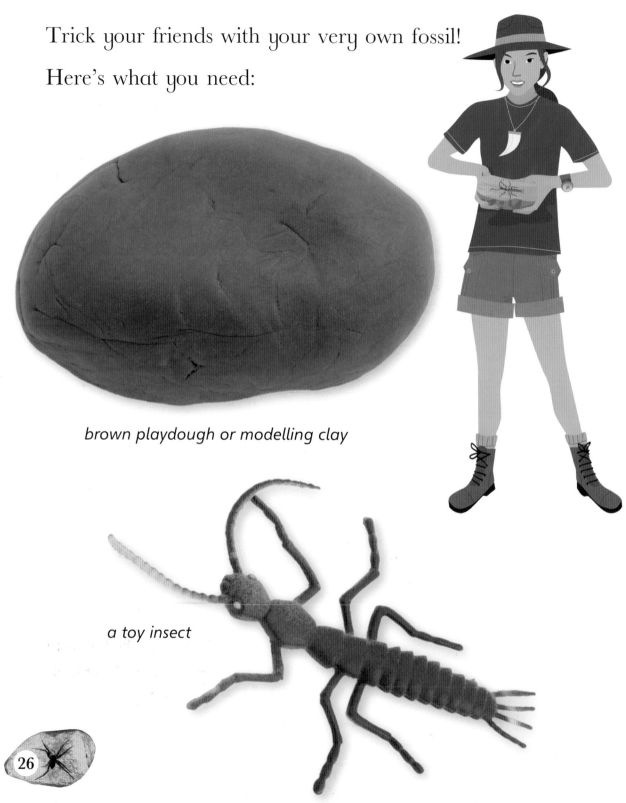

brown playdough or modelling clay

a toy insect

Here's what to do:

1. Roll the playdough into a ball.

2. Flatten the ball with your hand. Don't make it too thin.

27

3. Press your toy insect into the playdough. Then carefully pull it out of the dough. You will see the imprint left behind.

4. Put the dough in the sun to dry for a few hours.

Looks just like the real thing!

5. Now you have a fossil to show your friends!

29

Cool Fossil Facts

Fossils are great, aren't they?

a Barosaurus skeleton being assembled in a museum

Which Fossil Is This?

See if you can match the fossil with its name.

1. shark tooth   **4.** dinosaur tooth

2. fish   **5.** dinosaur bone

3. seashell

A

B

C

D

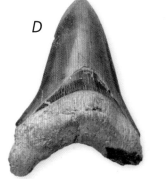

E

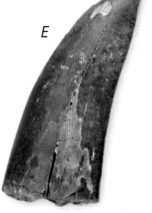

Answers: 1.D 2.C 3.A 4.E 5.B

Glossary

frozen fossils
dead animal or plant that has been in ice for a long time. A frozen fossil animal contains the animal's whole body, even its hair, skin and what's in its stomach.

imprint
mark or picture left behind in something such as mud

remains
what is left behind after a plant or animal dies

rot
when dead plants or animals break down into smaller parts

trace fossils
marks that have been left behind by an animal, that are turned into fossils, e.g. footprints, droppings, and even burrows and nests

woolly mammoth
large elephant-like animal that lived from about 120 000 to 4 000 years ago. They had long dark hair and long curved tusks, and ate plants.

Index